Pebble® Plus

Under the Sea
Sponges

by Jody Sullivan Rake

Consulting Editor: Gail Saunders-Smith, PhD

Consultant: Debbie Nuzzolo
Education Manager
SeaWorld, San Diego, California

Capstone press®

Mankato, Minnesota

Pebble Plus is published by Capstone Press,
151 Good Counsel Drive, P.O. Box 669, Mankato, Minnesota 56002.
www.capstonepress.com

1 2 3 4 5 6 11 10 09 08 07 06

Library of Congress Cataloging-in-Publication Data
Rake, Jody Sullivan.
    Sponges / by Jody Sullivan Rake.
    p. cm.—(Pebble Plus. Under the sea)
    Summary: "Simple text and photographs present the lives of sponges"—Provided by publisher.
    Includes bibliographical references and index.
    ISBN-13: 978-0-7368-6366-7 (hardcover)
    ISBN-10: 0-7368-6366-4 (hardcover)
    1. Sponges—Juvenile literature. I. Title. II. Series: Under the sea (Mankato, Minn.)
QL371.6.R35 2007
593.4—dc22   2005035967

Editorial Credits
Mari Schuh, editor; Juliette Peters, set designer; Patrick D. Dentinger, book designer; Kelly Garvin,
        photo researcher/photo editor

Photo Credits
Jeff Rotman, 11
Minden Pictures/Norbert Wu, 20–21
PhotoDisc Inc., back cover
Seapics/Andrew J. Martinez, cover; Doug Perrine, 6–7, 13, 17
        Marilyn and Maris Kazmeers, 19
Shutterstock/Dennis Sabo, 1
Tom Stack & Associates Inc./Therisa Stack, 8–9, 14–15; Tom Stack, 5

Note to Parents and Teachers

The Under the Sea set supports national science standards related to the diversity
and unity of life. This book describes and illustrates sponges. The images support early
readers in understanding the text. The repetition of words and phrases helps early
readers learn new words. This book also introduces early readers to subject-specific
vocabulary words, which are defined in the Glossary section. Early readers may need
assistance to read some words and to use the Table of Contents, Glossary, Read More,
Internet Sites, and Index sections of the book.

Table of Contents

What Are Sponges?

Sponges are animals

that look like plants.

Sponges grow into

many shapes and colors.

5

Some sponges are
as big as a person.
Other sponges are
as small as a ladybug.

Body Parts

Small holes called pores
cover a sponge's body.
Water flows into the pores.

9

Hairs inside sponges
pick out bits of food
from the water.

11

Then the water flows
out of large holes
on a sponge's body.

What Sponges Do

Sponges stick to rocks

on the ocean floor.

15

Animals eat

parts of sponges.

The sponges regrow

the missing parts.

Some animals

live inside sponges.

Sponges keep

these animals safe.

Under the Sea

Many different sponges

live under the sea.

Glossary

flow—to move smoothly and continuously

plant—a living organism that can make its own food from the sun's energy; sponges look like plants, but they are animals because they don't make their own food.

pore—a tiny hole on the skin or outer covering of an animal

Read More

Logue, Mary. *Sponges.* Science Around Us. Chanhassen, Minn.: Child's World, 2005.

Morgan, Sally. *Sponges and Other Minor Phyla.* Animal Kingdom. Chicago: Raintree, 2005.

Stone, Lynn M. *Sponges: Science Under the Sea.* Rourke Discovery Library. Vero Beach, Fla.: Rourke, 2003.

Internet Sites

FactHound offers a safe, fun way to find Internet sites related to this book. All of the sites on FactHound have been researched by our staff.

Here's how:

1. Visit *www.facthound.com*

2. Choose your grade level.

3. Type in this book ID **0736863664** for age-appropriate sites. You may also browse subjects by clicking on letters, or by clicking on pictures and words.

4. Click on the **Fetch It** button.

FactHound will fetch the best sites for you!

Index

Word Count: 102
Grade: 1
Early-Intervention Level: 12